In the

by Isabel Johnson

 HOUGHTON MIFFLIN   BOSTON

PHOTOGRAPHY CREDITS: Cover © Robert Maier/Animals Animals Earth Scene; Toc © Markus Botzek/zefa/CORBIS; 2 © Markus Botzek/zefa/CORBIS; 3 © Richard Day/Animals Animals Earth Scene; 4 © B. Runk/S. Schoenberger/Grant Heilman; 5 © Robert Maier/Animals Animals Earth Scene; 6 © Digital Vision/Veer

Printed in China

ISBN-13: 978-0-547-01853-9
ISBN-10: 0-547-01853-3

15 16 17 18 0940 20 19 18 17
4500634148

Birds like the garden.

Bees like the garden.

Bugs like the garden.

Worms like the garden.

I like the garden.

Responding

TARGET SKILL **Sequence of Events** This book tells about a garden. Tell the order in which things are described in the story. Make a chart.

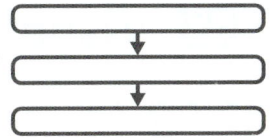

✏️ Write About It

Text to Self What things have you seen in a garden? Draw a picture of a garden. Label the things in your picture.

WORDS TO KNOW

all | she

TARGET SKILL **Sequence of Events** Tell the order in which things happen.

TARGET STRATEGY **Visualize** Picture what is happening as you read.

GENRE **Informational text** gives facts about a topic.